TIME FOR KIDS READERS

Homes

by Ellen A. Goodenow

Harcourt
SCHOOL PUBLISHERS

Orlando   Austin   New York   San Diego   Toronto   London

Visit *The Learning Site!*
www.harcourtschool.com

A home can be large.

A home can be small.

A home can be round.

A home can be square.

A home can be in the city.

A home can be in the country.

What is your home like?